How to get rich

How to make money with these business models.

Daniel A. Reedman

Table of Contents

INTRODUCTION 5

CHAPTER ONE 7

    INSTRUCTIONS TO MAKE MONEY ONLINE WITHOUT INVESTMENTS 7

    HOW TO MAKE MONEY ONLINE WITHOUT INVESTMENT 10

    TIME TESTED METHODS TO MAKE MONEY ONLINE WITHOUT INVESTMENT 15

    EXTRAORDINARY TOP-NOTCH WAYS TO MAKE MONEY ONLINE WITHOUT INVESTMENT! 20

CHAPTER TWO 22

    4 BLOGGING STRATEGIES ON HOW TO MAKE MONEY ONLINE WITHOUT INVESTMENT 22

    THE BEST TECHNIQUE TO MAKE MONEY ONLINE WITHOUT INVESTMENT - HOW SEO IS A GREAT OPTION AND FREE 25

    HOW TO MAKE MONEY ONLINE WITHOUT INVESTING MUCH .. 27

    MAKE MONEY ONLINE WITHOUT INVESTING 29

    HOW TO START A BLOG AND MAKE MONEY 31

CHAPTER THREE 35

    5 INTERNET MARKETING STRATEGIES TO PROMOTE YOUR GRAPHICS DESIGN BUSINESS 35

    BEGINNING A WEB DESIGN BUSINESS - WHAT YOU NEED TO KNOW 38

    ONLINE COURSES 41

    THE INSTAGRAM MARKETING STRATEGY FOR SUCCESS 43

    DIGITAL BROADCAST BUSINESS - 5 STEPS TO SUCCESSFUL PODCASTING 45

AMAZON MARKETPLACE AND EBAY STRATEGIES - STRATEGIC BOOK-BUYING FOR EASY RESALE 47

CHAPTER FOUR 50

HOW TO START YOU OWN PHONE ACCESSORY BUSINESS 50

PARTNER SALES AND MARKETING - HOW TO GET STARTED 51

SETTING YOUR OWN VIRTUAL ASSISTANT BUSINESS 53

KEYS TO HOME TAX PREPARATION BUSINESS SUCCESS - AFFORDABLE AND EFFECTIVE MARKETING 55

ONLINE NETWORKING MANAGEMENT - A MUST FOR YOUR BUSINESS 56

BUILDING YOUR INTERNET MARKETING CONSULTANT BUSINESS 59

CHAPTER FIVE 61

POINTS OF INTEREST OF HAVING A CONSULTING BUSINESS 61

INSIDE DESIGN CONSULTANTS 64

REALISTIC REASONS TO START A HOUSESITTING BUSINESS 66

SITTER SERVICES - FINDING BABYSITTERS MADE EASY 68

THE MOST EFFECTIVE METHOD TO RUN A PROPERTY MANAGEMENT BUSINESS 70

ANALYZING YOUR EBAY SALES 71

SELLING THROUGH ETSY 73

WEB BUSINESS TIPS - HOW CAN I INCREASE SALES OF FIVERR GIGS? 76

HOW TO BE A GREAT PORTRAIT PHOTOGRAPHER 78

CHAPTER SIX 80

VOCATION AS A WEDDING PHOTOGRAPHER 80

THE BEST STRATEGY TO MAKE MONEY ONLINE WRITING AND SELLING EBOOKS 83

GREETING CARDS FOR A HOME BASED BUSINESS 86

EVERYBODY CAN SELL ART ONLINE 88

PROVIDING FOOD BUSINESS 90

CHAPTER SEVEN 92

EARN A LIVING BUYING AND SELLING DOMAIN NAMES 92

ACQUIRE EXTRA CASH PROOFREADING AND EDITING FOR ONLINE COMPANIES 94

STARTING A YOUTUBE CHANNEL 96

HOW TO BUILD WEALTH 97

HOW TO CREATE WEALTH WITHOUT MONEY 102

CONCLUSION 108

INTRODUCTION

Numerous people seek to make money online, and it is an incredible inclination when one makes money online without spending a pie for a reason. Indeed, even with no product accessible for business, one can make money online. Anyway, one threat while striving for this is the tricks online that is qualification point between the promotion and genuine articles.

Competitors endeavoring to find how to make online frequently see that the guarantees established in the promotions for getting money online finish in disaster because of the way that those arrangements don't convey any fact in them. That is the reason numerous people make an inquiry whether some other individuals aside from the specialists make money on the Internet and that too with no real investments.

Uplifting news for such wannabes who want to make money online through business advancement or advancing the products and services is that it is conceivable. One of the ways of earning online is playing lotto recreations or gambling clubs online. In any case, it is essential choosing a company that would pay money and not merely the focuses as remunerations. Else the company should offer opportunities to win money.

While advancing products, it would be reasonable choosing a company that does not require any hard selling. The idea of affiliate marketing has gotten in a significant way. Rather than selling products, it includes just referral services. The advertiser only alludes the products to imminent customers, and the company pays them for such referral services. While the money earned through affiliate marketing isn't much when taken unit astute, it could signify considerable sums when taken together. Regardless, the company that gives excellent profits for the time contributed should be an ideal company to work with.

In the meantime, the online company to work with ought to be real. It won't be the best of the encounters getting engaged with prosecution endeavoring to gain money. A genuine company will enable one to win money helpfully online.

Two different ways of advantageously procuring money online could be associating planned bosses with forthcoming workers and imminent purchasers with imminent venders. Both can be great methods for gaining money online, and the end profit could be significant.

Chapter one

Instructions to Make Money Online Without Investments

The internet has altered from being a data asset instrument to an amusement source lastly to a money printing asset. If your month to month profit is insufficient to provide food for your necessities, at that point, you can swing to the internet where you will make money online without investments. There are a few websites which won't just illuminate you on the best way to make money yet additionally present you with the employment to or money-making plans. Such sites include:

- Money online.we.bs
- ForeclosureCash.net
- OvernightCashSystem.com
- Asiawriters.com
- SurveyMoneyMachine.com

The numerous ways through which you can make money online are checked on beneath:

1. Compose online articles for pay

There are heap sites that will only expect you to compose articles of your zone of claim to fame which you submit to get paid. Such sites incorporate Helium, eHow, WikiHow, and numerous others. The system for signing up is straightforward as you will need to sign up with their "Journalists Compensation Program." How great the articles that you compose will decide the number of people that visit the site to peruse the article. Related adverts are incorporated on the article page, and you procure by the name of snaps created on that page. Different places worth considering are Associated Content, Bukisa, and HubPages.

2. Partaking in online surveys

Numerous organizations don't need to take physical surveys that include polls. Preferably, they employ online Survey Companies that survey for their sake. Such organizations include:

- Ipsos I-state
- Global Test Market
- My Survey
- My View and
- Opinion Outpost

It is pivotal that you join sites that are entirely looked into through part signed in surveying online journals. Some places can hold you at payment with reformatory end client understanding terms that you need to set aside some effort to take a gander at explicitly. They are always persuaded that numerous people who register at these sites never set aside some effort to survey the terms and conditions.

3. Profiting through online journals and websites

Sign up at free blogging sites. An elective way is to design your very own website. You should think of innovative a point that keeps perusers returning for progressively content. Along these lines, your adverts can collect enough snaps to warrant your installment. Add Google AdSense to enable you to make money.

Professionals

Profiting online requires practically zero investment. All you need is a PC and an active internet association. Furthermore, you can do it nearby your first employment.

Cons

On the other side, profiting online necessitates that you register with such vast numbers of sites which can be challenging to oversee in addition to the likelihood of being misled.

How to Make Money Online Without Investment

A few people still feel that it is difficult to make money online starting with no outside help however given me a chance to disclose to you that there is an approach to make money online without contributing a single penny.

So what is this technique?

This is tied in with composing articles at specific spots. You possess every one of the rights to your materials as a rule, and you continue acquiring from an article a seemingly endless amount of time after a year. This won't make you rich immediately; however, whenever done custom, you can begin making automated revenue which continues expanding with time and the effort you put in. Individuals do make over a thousand bucks for every month composing articles continually quite a long time after a month. Presently there is a generally great rundown of such sites which you can discover by following the association given after this chapter. You should merely join on these websites as a part, picked a subject to write an article, write an article on that point and you are finished. You will win money from the advertisements shown in your items. These promotions are ordinarily AdSense, Amazon, eBay and so on. Generally, there is a part of the salary to support you.

Some helpful hints

Do whatever it takes not to get fretful. Even though these websites are excellent and articles composed there rank high in search engines, yet at the same time the materials you will write may set aside some effort to get ordered in search engines and bring traffic. So persistence is the key.

Endeavor to get a couple of backlinks towards your articles from different websites. Additionally, interlink your items that are identified with one another. Have a go at utilizing many stay content while connecting.

Try not to duplicate the articles. Write unique substance for best outcomes.

Research Search Engine Optimization (SEO) and execute it.

Incorporate related recordings and pictures in your articles.

At long last, good luck for your vocation of profiting online.

Will You Make Money Online Without Investment?

Each man's fantasy is to make a lot of riches, and to create a wealth; you have to contribute a ton of riches. No business is free of investment. Investment as money is one of the pre-requisite for any company. Different investments are like time and effort. So is it extremely conceivable to make money online without investment?

A poor man's business is based on dreams. He doesn't have the cash-flow to contribute and begin a business. So his creative energy is around starting a company with no investment.

This creative ability is at long last ending up valid on the internet. You would now be able to begin an online business with no investment and make money online.

So what is an online business and how might it be managed without investment?

An online business is a business that is done on the internet. The vehicle of collaboration between the company and the clients is the internet. There are trillions of products and administrations that are sold on the internet regularly.

With the coming of innovation and the development of the internet, the world has contracted, and business currently has no limits. Somebody in the United States would now be able to pitch online to somebody who is remaining in the Philippines. This has opened up open doors for everybody around the globe.

Even though I said that you could make money online without investment, I should marginally differ with myself here and state that in actuality there is some investment required.

Try not to stress; it isn't money that you should contribute. The investment in an online business is as time and effort. You should add a touch of time and part of shots if you are to assemble an online store. An online business expects you to be steady and industrious in your efforts.

For what reason doesn't an internet marketing business require any financial investment?

Let us first see what is required for an internet marketing business -

1) A website

2) A product to sell

3) Acquire clients willing to purchase

4) Payment engine to charge clients

You won't require something else to maintain an online business. What's more, the truth is that you won't have to contribute a single penny on any of the above things.

Making a website involves a couple of snaps nowadays. There are a large number of sites that let you create site pages and complete websites. The place like Squidoo.com, Hubpages.com will give you a chance to build a one-page site on any subject, and you can advance your product on this page. Some different sites like Tumblr.com and Blogger.com let you create whole websites as online journals. You can sell anything you desire on these websites.

What product will you sell? The most straightforward product to market is a data product. Individuals are searching for answers for their issues, and it is incredibly simple to create a data product offering a solution for these issues.

If you would prefer not to invest energy making a product, you could settle on affiliate marketing and sell other individuals' products for a commission.

Obtaining clients, at the end of the day getting traffic is a standout amongst the most troublesome things in internet marketing. In any case, it is simple if you pursue some spread out fundamental advances. Bum marketing is one of the most straightforward approaches to produce traffic and that too with no investment.

If you are into affiliate marketing, you won't require a payment engine. In any case, if you are selling your very own product, you will for sure need a payment engine. One alternative that does not require any investment is Google Checkout.

Time Tested Methods To Make Money Online Without Investment

It has happened to us all to discover one of those spam messages about how to make thousands of dollars a month with at least exertion. Among the limitless tricks you can find on the Internet, there genuinely are some straightforward and successful strategies that can enable you to make money online without investment.

Luckily, there are sheltered and legitimate ways to earn money on the Internet, yet every one of them requires a great deal of exertion and assurance from your part. One thing is without a doubt: if you get an "Irresistible Offer" that professes to enable you to make thousands of dollars daily, that is in all respects liable to be tricky and you ought to stay away from it. If something sounds pipe dream, it most likely is!

Taking affiliate marketing, for instance, this is a protected and lawful way to make money online without investment. If you have great marketing abilities and you need to advance another person's administrations or products, at that point affiliate marketing might be actually what you need. As a rule, this sort of marketing includes posting a connection on your site - you will consequently earn a commission at whatever point a guest makes a buy through your link. You should not merely to locate an essential organization with a mainstream product and advance it!

Then again, drop shipping another option that might be certainly justified regardless of your time and your consideration, if you need to make money online without investment. More or less, with drop shipping, you can go without much of a stretch sell products by going about as a middle person among dealer and purchaser. If you consider considering drop shipping, at that point peruse the Internet for some reputable and reliable discount organizations. In any case, check the reputation alongside the available installment options before agreeing to accept an organization.

If you don't prefer to take your risks with regards to making money online without investment, at that point, you ought to unquestionably think about online auctions. Fundamentally, you should only to join with the online closeout, post an image alongside a point by point product depiction and the offering will begin immediately. You should deal with subtleties, for example, shipping, however making money with online auctions is unquestionably an extraordinary thought!

If you are sufficiently inventive, you can even make your very own product or concoct a different online administration. If you need to make money online without investment, you can turn into an independent author, picture taker or visual planner. For this situation, you will pitch your administrations and products to different organizations in the online condition.

Outsourcing is without a doubt an incredible option when you need to be autonomous and possess enough energy for yourself. If you become a consultant, you will see how to maintain a business and whether you are prepared to stop your office occupation and begin a business all alone.

To condense, recollect that "Exploration" is the catchphrase if you consider making money online. There are many ways to deal with benefit on the web without investment and in a protected, legitimate way. Then again, many tricks are prowling around also. If you are resolved and you have the stuff, you can even earn an unfaltering, full-time salary from the security of your own home!

Instructions to Make Money Online Without Investment Starting Today

This part will impart to you how to make money online without investment. Everybody needs to earn "internet money." The ideal way is to do this is with no experience and with zero expense. Envision this; you could have different wellsprings of online payment. This will build your floods of pay. Dispose of the fantasy that you need to claim a site, you should have the online product to sell, or you should procure the specialized aptitudes or "internet sharp" for you're to earn "internet money."

You could even now earn "internet money" if you are not a website specialist or a marketing virtuoso. You are as yet thinking about how to make money online without investment? Investigate the accompanying ways.

1. Online Writing

You could unquestionably earn "internet money" if you cherish composing. There are article indexes or sites which pay you money if you submit or contribute your composition to them. Investigate these destinations, for instance, Helium, Hubpages, Squidoo, Snipsly and Info Barrel. Begin composing and sharing and begin making money online without investment.

2. Affiliate Marketing

This is the best online business show for an apprentice online advertiser. Fundamentally, you advance some else's product online, and you get paid a commission by effectively done as such. You could get the affiliate products for nothing at the affiliate systems. You could utilize article marketing or notwithstanding blogging to advance the affiliate products.

3. Blogging

You don't need to have a site, and you don't need to think about web planning for you to set-up and blog. You could even set up a blog for nothing inside minutes and begin posting. Spot promotions for nothing on your blog and you will get paid when the guests click on the advertisements. You could even place your affiliate interface on your blog and advance the affiliate product through your blog. Once more, share your story, your enthusiasm or whatever intriguing themes through your blog and earn money online without investment.

How to make money online without investment? Investigate the above now and incorporate online composition, affiliate marketing, and blogging and begin making "internet money." If it isn't brilliant for you to have the capacity to earn money online without contributing a solitary dime?

Extraordinary Top-Notch Ways to Make Money Online Without Investment!

There are a variety of options out there for making money online, yet there are not all that numerous out there that enable you to make money online without investment. The vast majority who are searching for an authentic way to make money online either swing to a type of online marketing or another kind of online business. There are just not excessively numerous things out there that don't expect you to make a generous investment to begin. If you resemble other people needing to get their foot off the ground with another business, There are diverse ways to deal with the benefit on the web now and then perplexing to come up with cash to start things up. You are likely going in an industry to profit since you need it-not to consume money.

You are now and again encountering specific undertakings that help members to find specific items to market can be an exceptional method to profit online without venture. You can discover particular details on the web and exhibit them to other individuals and influence a rate for each arrangement you to make. There is a tremendous amount of cash to be made here of business online. When you are thinking about it, you ought to never forget that you should concentrate on the product and make beyond any doubt that you get it out before whatever number people as could be expected under the circumstances. You additionally need to make people need the product, which can be more earnestly than it appears.

If this isn't the kind of online business that you are keen on, there are different ways to make money online without investment. Set aside the effort to investigate a portion of different options that are accessible to you. You ought to think about what it is that you like to do and discover something that will suit your loving just as your monetary needs. There is no reason that you ought to need to set up money in advance to work together online.

Begin your business today, and learn how to make money online without investment. There are numerous open doors simply hanging tight to be overturned. Set aside the effort to locate the ones that will work out best for you. There are some that don't require a great deal of time be put into it. You merely need to make sense of what you need to put into it and do things that way that you need them done.

Time To Pay Close Attention!

Vast amounts of money can be made on the Internet once you take a few to get back some composure of the correct data. Numerous Marketers including myself are making a decent living on the internet and will keep on doing all things considered for an extensive time allotment to come.

Chapter two

4 Blogging Strategies on How to Make Money Online Without Investment

Making money will be simple if you use blogging. Blogging is one of the least complicated ways to make money online without venture. You merely need to do work straightforwardly with consistency. Thus, here are the best blogging methodologies you can apply on your blog and make good online money at home.

Blogging strategy # 1: Involve in PCC publishing or Affiliate Program

To begin with, every one of you needs to include in any PCC publishing or affiliate program, because both are the most ordinary and effective ways to make money from blogging. Google AdSense is the best PCC publishing program, yet in case you are not acknowledged by Google, at that point attempts other AdSense options like Chitika, Yahoo Publisher, and numerous others. What's more, the most popular affiliate program is controlled by ClickBank. Go to ClickBank and be an affiliate. If you are inexperienced with PCC publishing and affiliate advertising, at that point, you need to find out about this. You may make money without knowing the two programs.

Blogging Strategy # 2: Do some keyword research

Before composing and posting an article at your blog you need to research a few keywords since keywords are the searched words. If you know which keywords are popular and less in the rivalry, you will almost certainly compose for hungry groups. My most loved keyword tool is Google AdWord Keyword Tool. Go at this keyword tool and type your specialty. You will get 50 to 100 outcomes. Get a few keywords which have 10,000 to 5,000 worldwide search volumes. Also, attempt to compose for those keywords. It will get a higher position at Google and more traffic.

Blogging Strategy # 3: Write for long tail keywords

Utilizing long tail keywords is the best way to get more focused on gathering of people. In case you don't have the foggiest thought what long tail keywords are, I propose you to find out about it. For this, you type 'The long Tail Keywords' on Google, and it will raise a large number of results.

Blogging Strategy # 4: Spread Your Back-joins

It is a standout amongst the essential pieces of blogging. Spreading back-joins is the way to get higher page rank on search motors since search motor robots discover how popular your blog is. What's more, if they find out your blog has loads of back-joins, they will rank you higher in their search pages. Lastly, you will get more search for motor traffic.

Some practical ways to spread back-joins are:

- Compose something like one article day by day and submit to top 10 article registries with your back-joins.

- Go to Yahoo Answers and pick a few inquiries related with your specialty and begin giving answers with your back-joins.

- Keep in touch with specific advertisements for your blog. Offer something free. What's more, post those promotions on top free classifieds like Craigslist, My space characterized and numerous others.

The best technique to Make Money Online Without Investment - How SEO Is a Great Option and Free

Understanding and actualizing search motor enhancement or SEO is an excellent free strategy to drive heaps of traffic to your website and increment deals which is how to make money online without venture. The objective of SEO is to get your online business on the main page of Google inside the leading ten rankings of the primary page. Doing this will enable vast amounts of traffic to your business since it's what individuals will search for anyways and it doesn't cost anything if you know the correct procedures. Here are a few hints on executing SEO and expanding your Google rankings:

Specialty. It is vital to discover a hobby or market to shape an online nearness in. Website design enhancement is tied in with beginning little and explicit and after that getting to be full as you increment your notoriety. Discover a market that isn't excessively focused however where you can likewise be produced. You need to begin off with something extraordinary; yet not all that one of a kind that individuals are not by any stretch of the imagination searching for it and purchasing anything.

Keyword research. This is very frequently disregarded and likely generally essential. It is imperative to comprehend which keywords to upgrade while advancing your business. Excessively focused on keywords, and you'll be disappointed and not get an opportunity. Any unbeneficial keywords and you'll have numerous searches however no deals and make no money. So it's crucial to you utilize free tools, for example, Google's keyword tool for a guide to dissecting which keywords merit seeking after and using.

Back connections. Another critical technique when you need to realize how to make money online without the venture is making back connections. What this is our site pages indicating and connecting back your very own website. For instance, you may post your relationship on a wide range of blog destinations and discussions. Along these lines, Google will perceive your site as being "popular" and give some expert to your site expanding its rankings.

Content. It's imperative to have excellent quality content on your online business or website to support its Google rankings. You need to have your keywords all through your website's content and have one of a kind recordings and media also. Likewise having fantastic content will expand your business transformation and consistency standards. Individuals need to feel increasingly good when something is of high caliber as opposed to something that has poor content and looks amateurish with poor syntax and random subjects and items. Thus, it is critical to have the best possible direction, preparing, and instruction with regards to figuring out how to make money online without speculation.

How to Make Money Online Without Investing Much

Many individuals have reached me to solicit what type from spending they ought to have put aside to go into business so they can begin making money online. In all actuality you need about $20 or less - read on to discover why.

The most critical piece of endeavoring to make money online is to have your very own website. This isn't the primary way; however, it is the most beneficial. You can enroll an area name and set up some web facilitating for considerably less than $20, and if you get fortunate with rebate coupons, you can do it for almost free.

In reality, you can do it entirely for nothing - there are many democratic administrations online that will let you set up your very own web space without paying. If you are not kidding about making money, at that point, you will need to get your very own website address. This is fundamental to look proficient.

You cannot make money anyway just by making a website. A standout amongst the best ways is by utilizing your site as an affiliate. This implies you can make some money by offering items that don't have a place with you. This is splendidly real and most expansive online stores have affiliate programs. When you sell the things you are advancing, the shipper that claims the item will give you a specific level of the selling cost.

It is additionally liberated to be an affiliate. You can enlist on individual websites or to a branch arrange, the last giving you substantially more decision on what you can advance.

This part is tied in with making money online without spending much. As should be obvious, it ought to be shoddy. There are no pyramid schemes so you should work at it and keep your website refreshed however if you are not kidding, at that point this won't be an issue.

Make Money Online Without Investing

One of the snappiest creating ways to make money is using the Internet; however, with regards to online, you may be timid away from the idea at first. In any case, it is an incredible way to make money without the need to contribute cash or have an internet business. Let's be honest, when you need to earn money, you are in no situation to add anything, and there are numerous ways you can win money legitimately without each contributing a penny.

Numerous people, perhaps you, think there is some enormous equation to make money online and that it is confounded and most likely costly, yet this isn't valid. You can take a portion of the aptitudes you have now and use them on the Internet to earn money. For example, would you say you are right at math and science, and people regularly come to you when they need assistance with their homework? Did you know numerous organizations will pay you on an independent premise to coach online?

This is one of the following immense endeavors of multiple programs is to help coach children, and you don't just have a showing accreditation as a rule.

Have you worked in an office as a clerical specialist? Provided that this is true, presently you could fill in as an independent remote helper. It is an exceptionally regular position to see nowadays because those that do have an Internet business can't do everything that is required and in this manner, they employ remote helpers to take on a portion of the heap. You can earn money and work from your home on the Internet, which is a success win circumstance for you! Check a part of the independent employment destinations, and you will locate a few remote helper positions. Numerous people function as full-time remote helpers and make a better than average pay in the meantime.

Do you want to do look into online and would you say you are good at discovering data? You probably won't understand it, yet various organizations employ people to do online research. You can make money and accomplish something straightforward for you. Also, you don't need to have an Internet business in the first place, yet if it is something you need to transform into a trade later then you unquestionably can and should start a website.

At last, the thing to remember when you need to make money online is to pick something simple for you.

Choosing something that takes you hours for only a smidgen of pay, won't merit your time. Start gradually, and make money rapidly and attempt several roads, when you discover something you are good at and earning good money, at that point, you will need to open your very own internet business.

How To Start A Blog And Make Money

You have seen it in motion pictures and on TV and in the news: individuals selling their web journals, making them into books, making them into films, and when all is said in done only making cash off the web through blogging. Also, presently, you are intrigued as well! This part will give you the official lowdown on the most proficient method to make cash blogging.

To begin with, comprehend that all web advertising frameworks pursue three fundamental advances.

Discover an item to sell

Make your web nearness (for example blog)

Drive web site traffic to your online site or nearness

Pretty much every web-promoting model pursues these three stages. Conceded there are numerous approaches to pursue these three stages, however knowing from the begin that these are the three stages to achieve causes you remember the 10,000-foot view as you put your head down to begin your online business.

Presently with regards to making cash blogging, there are two different ways general approaches to do it: sell a specialty item (for example, dog training digital book) or market yourself as an item. In either case, you are beginning a blog to be your online nearness. If you are selling a specialty type item, we would call that a Niche Blog or Product Blog. On the off chance that you are selling yourself, at that point we would call that a Personal Blog. Both blogging models can fit directly into the over three-stage framework.

Individual Blog. Here is the way your three stages would work out:

Discover something to blog about. This could be a particular specialty (for example dog training), or it could be a wide range of specialties: anything you desire to express your sentiment about. One day it could be about different high definition TVs, the following day it could be about a child.

Compose your blog entry. Composing blog entries reliably, express every 4 to 7 days, will develop an extraordinary web nearness

Drive traffic to your blog. You could have the best blog on the planet, yet individuals need to realize how to discover it. This includes the specialty of backlink building. There are numerous approaches to fabricate backlinks, and you need to use a wide assortment of them.

Specialty Blog System and the three web-promoting steps:

Pick an item you need to sell (for example dog training manual), OR pick a specialty you are keen on (for example dog training) and you can choose the items later

Blog about points in your specialty, which assembles your online nearness.

Drive traffic to your blog site. This includes backlink building, like what was examined previously. The more connections and the more extensive assortment of, the better. Also if you can get joins from sites explicit to your specialty, that will be incredible as well.

Regardless of whether you make a Personal Blog or a Niche Blog, when you get moving and get perusers, it is genuinely simple to profit. The more traffic, the more cash. You can put promotion pennants on your blog, place Google AdSense advertisements on your blog, and partner item interfaces on your blog. Additionally, with each blog entry, you can likely discover an associated item or connection identified with that blog entry. The things will fluctuate for Personal Blogs since your themes will shift. For a Niche Blog, you can practice and keep on stopping a similar item (for example, your preferred dog training manual for a dog training blog).

Also, it's as simple as that. Basic? Indeed obviously it is. Simple? It requires significant investment and can even be very monotonous to develop a business. In any case, this is a framework pursued by numerous individuals to profit online with blogging. I trust that has provoked your interest and has helped you understand how it is quite easy to benefit on the web, profit on the internet, and make cash blogging. What's more, that now you also are thinking pretty much every one of the potential outcomes for yourself when you begin a blog.

Chapter three

5 Internet Marketing Strategies to Promote Your Graphics Design Business

Illustrations plan a decent redistributing business today. There is numerous professional illustrations fashioner doing this business on the web. This business is especially beneficial and demandable. The interest and chance of this business are expanding step by step. Be that as it may, some amateur illustrations originator can't get along admirably toward the start for the need for legal information on the web promoting. We will talk about the five most significant techniques of web showcasing to advance an illustrations structure business on the internet.

Web crawler showcasing

This is the most essential to begin and advance an illustrations plan business. To do this, open a decent website for your business. Select a whole catchphrase area for your website. Include your watchwords at related pages with new and real substance. Be careful! Try not to duplicate content from different sites. This will murder your website at birth. Presently do some SEO for your website making some high-quality backlinks. You can discover high-quality backlinks from gatherings, blog remarks, and composing articles. A little number of excellent backlinks to your site may expand the web crawler permeability of your website.

Online networking Marketing

When you are happy with your website content, begin advancing with online networking. Open a few profiles in high internet based life systems like Facebook, Twitter, Google+, LikedIn. Make a fan page of your business on Facebook and connection it with your website. You can make a business page in Google+ and LinkedIn as well. LinkedIn is particularly significant for elevating your business to professionals. See, the web-based life will be the most vital components to SEO and web promoting strategies in coming years. Along these lines, you may give the most need for online networking advertising. You can get some incredible thoughts from different advertisers following their systems. Increment your dynamic support in online networking sites, share substance normally, post refreshes, transfer pictures, and recordings post remarks, and so forth.

Email Marketing

Email advertising can assume a significant job to advance your illustrations structure business. To do this, you should assemble a rundown of potential clients. You can locate some incredible wellspring of email list from the web via search. I can likewise give you a wellspring of enormous measure of the focused rundown of messages. What's more, it stops the discussion spam website. Indeed, the review isn't of right individuals as they are recorded as spammers. You can likewise purchase an email list from brokers. I don't try the quality. Along these lines, I prescribe you to assemble your rundown in a usual manner permitting membership of guests from your website. Send messages to them with detail data of your items. Assume, for instance, your question is Photoshop Hair Masking. Include some photographs of test works of your administration and issues. You can offer some free administrations.

Target clients advertising

You can get potential clients for your Graphics plan or photograph altering business from different websites. Search for individuals or organizations who need your items and administrations. You can contact with the dealers on amazon.com or eBay.com and other comparable websites which have a massive amount of merchants with visual presentation of their items. They may require visual computerization or photograph altering administrations. Send individual messages with a short depiction of your administrations. You may discover a ton of right clients along these lines. If you find out any trouble, attempt again, and create your issues. You will end up fruitful in your business.

Consultant websites

Independent websites might be one of the significant wellsprings of customers. Register with a specialist, oDesk, guru.com, and some related sites. Assemble a professional profile and spot offers for related maintains and sources of income. It is challenging to land positions for learners from these websites. You should keep tolerance for all things considered.

Beginning a Web Design Business - What You Need to Know

1. Arranging

You should begin off with a strategy that is serviceable and reasonable. You have to distinguish your objective market dependent on the range of abilities you have, and your capacity to satisfy the tasks that may come to your direction. You have to consider whether more significant undertakings are the best, to begin with thinking about that beginning your own web plan business may mean your funds are in limbo for some time. A more drawn out undertaking may mean you need to hold up longer to get paid, except if you can arrange organized installments. You should likewise think about whether to go for a specialty advertise that suits your specific capacities or distinguish the administrations most looked for after by customers, and tailor your aptitudes to possess all the necessary qualities.

2. Business Acumen

Around half of all organizations bomb inside the initial five years. Because you don't have a shop or leasing office or any stock does not mean you are not maintaining a private company. Beginning your very own web plan business makes you just as defenseless to disappointment as anyone else if your business head isn't in a wrong way on the right. You should realize how to manage customers, bookkeepers, financiers, and skill to keep your business records in high request. Time-the executives and compromise are required abilities, and you should almost certainly adapt to stresses and due dates. The correct demeanor is urgent.

3. Web Authoring Tools

Web architects must probably make a straightforward web page by coding in HTML, yet you have to discover the web writing apparatuses that best suit how you work and the prerequisites of your working framework. Beginning your very own web structure business without the right devices for the activity is hoping the firearm.

4. Designs and Copyright Issues

You have to recollect that pictures and illustrations can't merely be winnowed off the web and utilized without idea. This could make you be in break of copyright laws and lead to perhaps extreme legitimate inconvenience. When you are not set up to dish out on sovereignty installments for pictures, you should have a prepared wellspring of allowed to-utilize images, for example, iStockPhoto, Royalty-Free Photos, or Photos.com.

5. Visual computerization Tools

As pictures and illustrations have such a significant impact in web structure, when beginning your very own web plan business, you should have appropriate designs altering programming. This ought to be fit for reason in that you should most likely make the impacts you need while not being bothered by a large group of users that are excessively unpredictable or extra for your own needs. Adobe Photoshop might be in this last classification, and it is costly so that you could glance around for an open-source alternative.

6. Legalities and Book-Keeping

This takes in such issues as illustration up contracts for your different ventures that spread the two gatherings, to dealing with your records. Beginning your own web structure business without getting your desk work all together leaves you open to a wide range of lawful and budgetary dirty tricks sometime later. On the off chance that this is a territory you are uncertain about, you are in an ideal situation paying legal advisors and bookkeepers to cover these employments. It is a false economy to hold back on these, go the do-it-without anyone else's help course, and discover you neglected something fundamental. Keep in mind additionally that you should frame a lawful business element to ensure yourself and make the most assessment productive circumstance for yourself.

Online Courses

Online courses are winding up mainstream. Most schools and colleges offer online courses either as degree courses or to enhance school training. Likewise, numerous Internet-based establishments provide online courses.

At the point when online courses are contrasted and ordinary homeroom courses, they are found to have the two favorable circumstances and disservices. The best favorable position that online classes give is adaptability. There is no set time for the course. The understudy can peruse the material and complete the assignments according to his or her comfort as long as it fits inside the general timetable. This is essential to the individuals who are working while at the same time taking the course. They can contemplate promptly in the first part of the day or late around evening time. Furthermore, they can do as such from their homes is an additional bit of leeway.

An inconceivable scope of online courses is accessible. They spread the standard subjects instructed in schools. Proficient online courses, (for example, portfolio the board) just as professional online courses are likewise accessible. One essentially needs to enter the subject in an internet searcher, and a rundown of sites offering the course will show up. Online courses are quickened courses. They are focussed and compacted and frequently set aside less effort to finish than regular classes.

The significant drawback of online courses is their adequacy by businesses and customary instructive foundations. Numerous courses are offered by sound associations and would be worthy; anyway, many would not. Thus if the online course is being taken for encouraging one's business potential or for picking up the entrance into a traditional school, its adequacy ought to be found out. The other issue with online courses is that they require a great deal of self-inspiration. The understudy isn't being administered on an everyday premise, and if the person neglects to turn in a task a zero would be given, and few inquiries would be posted.

The Instagram Marketing Strategy For Success

Posting At The Right Time

Timing is everything when using Instagram displaying. Your dedication depends upon your arranging. In case you post at a horrendous time, you may wrap up being unnoticed. Early morning or late around night time is the perfect time to post. Do whatever it takes not to post during or between the 9-5 business hours. The most exceedingly awful day for duty in seven days is Sunday while Monday and Thursday will, as a rule, have most raised Instagram supporter responsibility and traffic.

Seek after Similar Instagram Profiles

Seek after people who seek after a related interest you like. If you find individuals with similar interests, you will make sure to get took note. Besides, they will undoubtedly tail you back. Associate with people who you acknowledge would be excited about your things.

Get a Suitable Instagram Name

It is incomprehensible that people will examine for you by your name aside from if you are a VIP. So make names turning around your business site or the business that you are working in. By and by, when people related to your industry search the associated watchwords, almost certainly, your profile will appear. Here is an incredible Instagram promoting system. Make your "client name" indistinguishable from what you are selling since that is the thing that individuals are looking for.

Carefully Use The Description

When composing your depiction try to inform people regarding the upsides of you and your business. Add an association with your channel or advancing the effort to coordinate the general population on your page.

Add Texts To Images And Use Hashtags

Indeed, Instagram is more about pictures than plain messages. Including photos is an extraordinary method to tell individuals how brilliant your item or administration is. Utilize outwardly strong content that will stand out.

Everybody needs to use hashtags on Instagram, and if you need your business to be seen, by then, you have use hashtags. Utilizing hashtags will promise you to end up on the summary of the floating watchwords that people are checking for.

Digital broadcast Business - 5 Steps to Successful Podcasting

1) Setup your podcasting site first. Significantly, you make an alluring page for your podcasting. When you don't have the foggiest idea how to do this, you can generally employ somebody to do this for you. The page ought to dependably incorporate general data about your web recording. Moreover, it is imperative to place interfaces on your site page for your podcasting station to pick up a consistent progression of supporters of your feeds. You should likewise recall that the best web recording business dependably offers free material or data to make the endorser become continuous or approach the audience.

2) Get the space that you need. Since you have your podcasting website up and prepared, you have to set up some space on your web server that would store every

one of the documents that you expect to use in your podcasting. Ensure that the server you intend to utilize contains all the essential determinations that you may require.

3) Get the vital programming for your webcast business. You have to obtain fair projects that could assist you with your podcasting. This product may incorporate FTP move programs that will enable you to transfer your records over to your server. Top of the line encoders/decoders could help in giving quality music or recordings to suit your endorser's needs. In either case, the primary way you can keep up a profitable and fruitful podcasting business is by putting resources into devices that can add worth and imagination to your digital broadcast.

4) Advertise your administrations. The life of your digital broadcast business will rely upon the number of endorsers that you have. To do this, you need to appropriately spread out enough broad data about you and your webcast that will persuade a guest to buy into your digital broadcast sustains. Presenting joins on different destinations could build your endorsers too. It will demonstrate that you are propelled to give; however, much data and assets about the topic as could reasonably be expected.

5) Always update your digital broadcasts. It is useful for fruitful podcasting to refresh yourself on the most recent

innovation accessible to give the best administrations to your rundown of endorsers.

Amazon Marketplace and eBay Strategies - Strategic Book-Buying For Easy Resale

Need to look for books, read them and after that transform them once more into money by selling them on Amazon.com Marketplace? Perhaps you need to sell them on eBay. Peruse on to find which books to purchase (for resale) and which ones to get at the library (to peruse and return at no charge).

1) Stick with Non-Fiction (Mostly)

Right to life books has any more extended timeframe of realistic usability. Individuals discover them since they're keen on the subject. One particular case: If you purchase the new Harry Potter and you realize you can part with it inside half a month, you'll have the option to sell that rapidly also - and at a decent cost as well. Same for other prominent blockbusters. In any case, don't hold up excessively long - or else you'll have a surge of rivalry and the worth goes down to pennies.

2) Check Popularity of Book and Topic

When it's a hot merchant, there's a ton of pivot, so when you need to exchange your book, your odds are high that you can get a decent cost and it will sell rapidly.

3) Be Sure to Turn Your Books around Quickly

Try not to get them in mass (except if you can get an immense markdown). Purchase, read, and exchange. Quick. The quicker you exchange, the fewer contenders you'll have, and the higher the value you can get.

4) Treat Your Books VERY Well

Try not to peruse them over lunch or supper. Try not to stamp them in at any rate. If you can list your book as "like new" or if nothing else as "generally excellent," your odds are quite improved that somebody will get it, and at a decent cost as well. Indeed, anything less, and you should overlook it if there's any rivalry.

5) Go for Niche Books

Discover books in specialties that are sensibly well known (for quick turnover) however not stuffed. The odds are high that there'll be a constant flow of purchasers looking at your book.

6) Watch out for New Editions

When another release turns out, your book is useless. One more motivation to be speedy about separating with your papers by posting and selling them when you've perused them. Also, in case you're purchasing given resale, dependably get the most up to date release.

7) What about eBay?

With regards to selling books on eBay, the principles are comparative. For eBay, it's considerably progressively significant that your paper is perfect, except if you take an unmistakable photo of the majority of its flaws. Discussing picture... eBay can be much more work, and you need to pay posting charges, while at Amazon.com, you can use rundown books for nothing and possibly spend when you sell them.

Chapter Four

How to Start You Own Phone Accessory Business

When you are hoping to begin your very own phone accessory business, there are different things to consider and sorts of assistance to be viewed as sold. The extraordinary thing about this business is that the accessory world is developing and ending up progressively prevalent. Numerous individuals are not just content with their cell phone, yet additionally, need different physical accomplices to compliment it. All new generation phones have cutting edge innovations and utilizations which request assistants to be used.

Having the most prevalent physical embellishments is vital. Most of the phone clients will be looking through these out first, and this is likewise the most significant for them to boost the utilization of their phone. Defensive cases and screen defenders are exceptionally mainstream and significant. A few people like to have various hued situations and switch up the appearance of their phone. Additionally, see what adornments are one of a kind to prominent phone. A model is the LG treat, which has a wand accessible to all the more effectively utilize the touch screen innovation.

When investigating beginning up a phone accessory business, likewise observe what programming adornments or applications are sought after. If you can give these to the client, it will raise your deals and shot of rehash buys. Applications are gigantic in the iPhone world and other new-generation phones. There is a free Reign of Swords application for the iPhone, a computer game called the best system and the most no-nonsense of its sort for cell phones.

Discount cell phone embellishments are the best approach as individuals need the best reserve funds they can jump on their phone connections. Individuals will require a wide assortment of extras, from chargers to conveying cases, to vehicle bearers and numerous product updates and changes. By offering the most aggressive costs and administrations, you are en route to beginning a fruitful phone accessory business.

Partner Sales and Marketing - How to Get Started

Beginning in an associate showcasing program truly isn't as troublesome as you may suspect. These projects are intended to make it unbelievably simple for you to join and begin advancing their items and administrations immediately with almost no prior learning.

To start with, you need to discover a program. Utilize a web index, request proposals, or visit an offshoot program registry to get a thought of which plan you need to join. You may even need to search around a bit to see which one offers the best installments. Nothing says you can't join a few of them in case you're willing to put in twice or multiple times the work.

Joining most associate projects expects you to round out an online structure, yet these structures more often than not don't request much data. Regularly, you mostly snap join and make a record with the offshoot program. In any case, you more often than not require registration with one of the numerous online installment administrations like PayPal too. Most associate projects utilize these administrations to pay their individuals. When you don't have a record, it, as a rule, doesn't take too long to even think about setting one up, and most are allowed to join. Note, however, that a large number of these administrations take a little slice of any cash paid to you.

When you've joined, you should showcase the associate's program or item. This usually included sending a specific connection to other people. This connection incorporated your record data, so you get kudos for the sell. A few offshoots incorporate a layout to enable you to make a site publicizing their item. Some additionally offer illustrations, limited-time content, and other showcasing helps to allow you to get the message out about the subsidiary and make a decent measure of cash. Keep in mind, the all the more showcasing you do, the more money you'll make!

Setting Your Own Virtual Assistant Business

If you need to possess a virtual assistant business, you would need to think about the web and have a decent PC framework. If these two are set up, at that point, you would now be able to begin turning into a virtual assistant. The term virtual is an activity in a particular system. Assistant is a term that is clear as crystal. The two words joined will, without a doubt, give you a benefiting business.

Virtual help began in the '90s when online organizations began contracting assistants that would take a shot at their commercials. Before long, there is an interest in the increasingly real job. With the rise of the web, this should be possible with leaving home. The virtual assistant industry took off because business visionaries began propelling organizations that redistribute administrations. In the first years, the business was constrained to secretarial and administrative work. Today, this business can be considered as full time as individuals are being enlisted as self-employed entities. Some individuals are getting to be independently employed.

The virtual assistant can give administration is the littlest degree of business enterprise. Today it has a wide assortment of obligations and duties. They offer a progressively particular sort of business. There are different virtual assistant employments like money related assistants, admin, individual assistant, English mentor, preparing workforce, land, innovative, and even deals. This considered as a rewarding undertaking.

It is not hard to set up your very own virtual assistant business. It would require a ton of web information. It is ideal if you advance the administrations on the web. There is a virtual system where you can join and share the market. Commonly, you think about the internet since it is electronic. It is ideal when you can productively associate with your customers. A decent web association is an absolute necessity. This business adventure would require modem, links, and gear. Other works need webcams, speakers, and mic. This is the more significant part of your costs.

There are organizations with a specific set of working responsibilities. When you have the instruction and business-related aptitudes, it is ideal for maintaining the business from home. It pays to comprehend the obligations and duties given to you. It is perfect if you advance your organization that can enable you to get a consistent flow of work.

Keys to Home Tax Preparation Business Success - Affordable and Effective Marketing

Home-based tax preparation organizations need to concentrate on promoting methodologies significantly more vigorously than their retail customer-facing facade contenders and leading you to need a showcasing plan. Try not to believe that the majority of your loved ones will leave the woodwork at tax season and herd to your home to exploit your administrations.

Your advertising strategies should be gentler than a regular retail tax office, as you are ordinarily focusing on potential clients that you know or companions of individuals you know. A regularly disregarded promoting medium is online for interpersonal organizations. Pretty much everybody has known about Facebook and Twitter. When you are as of now using these instruments to keep in contact with loved ones, make sure to utilize it to tell them that your administrations are accessible to them. These are incredible mediums to achieve a general gathering of contacts inside your associated individual system. Try not to believe that it is inconsiderate or prominent to request clients for your home-based tax business. When you feel that way, you will be bankrupt before you know it. You should be particular about yourself and your capacity to give practical support of these customers and ought not to be embarrassed to advance yourself.

Offering your clients drop off administrations is another approach to separate your tax business from different alternatives out there. Be happy to get your customers' tax records and convey their profits to them, if that is progressively helpful for them. Most tax offices use a meeting sheet which gets most tax data required for finishing the individual bit of a tax return. Be quick and precise with your preparation and administrative work, to abstain from investing more energy in the street that would generally be appropriate. Numerous customers are email wise and are happy to give you the required data using scanner and email, and you can do a similar when conveying their arrival to them. You should make sure to keep up your IRS administrative work necessities, mainly when working a drop off tax administration. The IRS allows for advanced duplicates of e-document authorization signature pages, so email correspondence is worthy. Try to work your home-based business similarly as expertly as you would from a retail facade. Luckily since you are using a home office for your tax preparation business center, your costs ought to remain lower than the run of the mill retail tax office.

Online networking Management - A Must for Your Business

Advancing yourself or your business can be very tedious, particularly when it has to do with Facebook and Twitter. Two of the most intensely utilized web locales on the web are Facebook and Twitter. It is possible that you use them or you don't. Numerous individuals who utilize these specialized apparatuses for business have no clue how to utilize them appropriately and after that surrender too rapidly. There is an approach to help here. It is anything but difficult to procure somebody deal with your Facebook and Twitter accounts through online networking the executives.

An internet-based life the executive's organization can be utilized to support your organization or individual character develop on original locales, for example, Facebook and Twitter. They can discover you more fans or companions to speak with. They can likewise help with the everyday correspondences of your fans and supporters. This removes your hands from making posts day by day and considering daily tweets. It is an incredible help.

An internet-based life the executive's organization can likewise build up an advertising methodology that will support your Facebook and Twitter records detonate into a viral domain of progress. They will have thoughts, for example, how to showcase your Facebook page and Twitter account in the disconnected world. They can think of dreams, for example, printing your Facebook and Twitter pages on your receipts to having publications on your dividers with the tail our sign on the base. These thoughts are basic, yet decent online networking the board organization can concoct significantly increasingly innovative ideas.

A champion amongst the most troublesome errands of a Twitter and Facebook administrator is to keep your devotees glad and furthermore to interface with them consistently. An extraordinary web-based life the board organization will accomplish more than do day by day posts, they will likewise get your supporters to retweet for you to begin something viral and they will get individuals reacting to posts on your organization's Facebook divider. Online life is tied in with building up an association with your past and future clients. The more association your organization has, the more your organization will be recalled.

In general, taking care of these sorts of locales all alone is tedious. You need to experience the day by day errands of discovering Twitter devotees that will peruse your posts and Facebook fans that will like your business. Regardless of whether you have sufficient energy to do it, would you say you are building up the best possible promoting plan that has as a result on your main concern? A decent web-based life the board organization will help you in astonishing ways and increment your client base by setting up a never observed day by day relationship.

Building Your Internet Marketing Consultant Business

In these uncertain economic occasions, it's insufficient to be skilled. To get by in the stormy waters of the ebb and flow economy, you additionally must most likely observe a chance and hold onto it. Web marketing counseling is a development industry that offers capable journalists, creators, engineers, and sales reps - the extremely same individuals who large organizations have cut back, furloughed and generally trampled upon - a chance to use their aptitudes into a high-paid work from home business.

As a regularly expanding number of associations develop an online nearness, they're going to need assistance in proficiently and viable marketing their products and ventures on the web. This presents an open door for gifted individuals to assume responsibility for their predeterminations by exploiting their innovative abilities to offer organizations the administrations of an IM consultancy.

What Skills Do You Have?

In case you're as of now talented in deals, composing or visual depiction, you as of now have 75% of all that you have to dispatch an effective IM consultancy. The rest of the 25 percent includes learning a couple of things about marketing, site design improvement, needs examination, specialty look into, and a couple of Web website building abilities.

With a grip of the basics of these ideas and a little moxie on your part, you can without much of a stretch parlay your current abilities into an energizing new business where you're the supervisor.

The Freedom of Consulting

An energizing aspect concerning beginning an Internet marketing counseling business is that you control your predetermination. You set your hours. You choose what undertakings to seek after. What's more, you pick who you work for. With this opportunity comes greater obligation, however, for business people who are driven, trained, and skilled, the additional requests become difficulties to be enjoyed. As a result of the adaptability engaged with Web marketing counseling, you can work for large organizations or have an independent company consultancy.

There are indeed a large number of independent companies searching for somebody to demonstrate to them the route in private venture IM counseling. These organizations understand that the Web presents many open doors for propelling their message and getting their name out in the general population. Execution of this hypothesis is missing. Nonetheless, the same number of private ventures have burdensome, cockeyed Web destinations.

Do You Have Discipline?

You can make a fortune helping private companies retool and update these destinations to end up lean, mean marketing machines. Going into this profession takes self-control, a promise to client administration and innovativeness. However, the magnificence is that nearly anybody can gain proficiency with the aptitudes essential for this profession. All you need is the correct teacher.

Chapter Five
Points of interest of Having a Consulting Business

Counseling is a decent decision for some individuals, and here is a portion of its points of interest as a business.

1. You are paid for what you know, not what you do.

The work isn't physically requesting in the manner difficult task can be. You don't need to finish the venture yourself. You need to make the procedure evident to the people who are taking every necessary step with the goal that they can do it. You are a free, talking reference book. You are not a working drone.

2. The compensation every hour is astounding.

A business that needs your recommendation and information will consider the time you go through counseling with them essential. They are not going to employ you for all time when they need your insight for a brief span. However, they realize they need to make it worth your time and energy to do the counseling work. Organizations are happy to pay a lot of cash for somebody to deal with their counseling errands on a momentary premise.

3. You pick your days off.

If you have a counseling business, you have a lot of command throughout the days you work. When you have something anticipated a specific date, it is genuinely simple to operate your timetable around with the goal that you are off for that occasion. In counseling, you don't need to work each day since you are profiting when you do work. Your administrations are famous, and your solicitations to do the counseling on your decision of days will be heard.

4. The material costs are insignificant.

In a counseling business, you need cash for any movement you need to do. When you need apparatuses that you don't have, you should get those. If your apparel does not coordinate with your expert picture, you should refresh your closet. You may require a bookkeeping system, and you will likely need proficient obligation protection. You can telecommute, and you don't need to procure representatives except if your business will benefit from doing as such.

5. The prizes are fulfilling.

Other than cash, you will get numerous prizes from working in your counseling business. You will build up a system of business partners, conceivably over an enormous geological zone. You will have played a part in ventures that you can be pleased with. You will procure notoriety for being a noteworthy player in the counseling industry. The preferences are appealing to the point that more individuals are getting into counseling each year.

Inside Design Consultants

Be it your work environment, your home, or your business; we generally need our space to be the ideal blend of the style with the down to earth. As people, we are continually ready to update for our best of favorable position.

The equivalent goes with space we claim which we always needed to modify as indicated by our needs and prerequisites. Inside structuring is a dreadful parcel something other than painting your dividers, improving your furnishings and appropriate lighting and consequently it is smarter to draw in expert assistance which will likewise spare you from a ton of migraines.

Legitimate space the board is just conceivable by connecting with the inside plan experts who outwardly improve your interior space as well as look to streamline and blend the utilization to which the assembled condition will be out for. Albeit a few people believe that connecting with an inside structure advisor is a costly business yet actually it very well may be a decent planning choice that won't just assistance you set aside cash in amassing your space however will likewise enable you to spare a great deal of time as opposed to overseeing things without anyone else's input.

With heaps of innovativeness sprinkled on your insides, even your basic room can resemble a million dollar place. Employing an expert to make your space increasingly alluring, exceptional, and useful is an incredibly insightful venture. The answers for the area the board is helpful, upgrade the personal satisfaction and culture of the tenants and are stylishly alluring. The private space and its capacity profoundly organize an inside creators counseling. Proficient experts know about the best, and the most sensible items accessible in the market that can make incredible ponder in your area.

These specialists can enable you to stay away from the migraines regularly connected with re-demonstrating, extension, and insides work in general. When thinking about how to upgrade any inside space, it is critical to consider exactly what sort of style you need to fuse in the gave area. In this manner, the interior structure experts help you change your vision into reality by applying their inventive aptitudes to successful use for arranging your space. With the assistance of an internal structure specialist, you will find that there are numerous choices open to you to change your area into something progressively perfect for your needs.

Realistic Reasons to Start a Housesitting Business

Did you realize that you also can begin a house sitting business? This is a business anybody can start, paying little respect to age or training. If you instruct yourself, you can be fruitful at this undertaking too.

It would undoubtedly amaze you precisely what the number of individuals is searching for house sitter administrations to help them in dealing with their home while they are away. Numerous individuals are going on expanded excursions or work excursions and don't have anybody to care for their home. This can open up a universe of business open doors for you.

You can without much of a stretch exploit this by beginning your very own home sitting business. You can arrange the general population you have to who might be needing this administration just as supply the general population to finish the administration. For the most part, you'll need to find the people who need to do the house sitting just like the homes to relax, and you're ready to go.

There is a whole other world to it than that, there dependably is, correct? It'll set aside some effort to get this together and will in all probability require some time for you make a benefit on a housesitting business, yet you can when you choose to put your brain to it.

Recorded beneath are a portion of the reasons mortgage holders are searching for housesitters:

We live in a dangerous world; an open house left standing welcomes thefts. Along these lines, to help keep away from these numerous individuals contract a house sitting support of assistance, they discover legit individuals to watch their home.

Many individuals have pets and plants that will die whenever left for extensive, and this requires a house-sitters consideration too. To enable them to deal with these.

Numerous things can happen to a home whenever left unattended. For example, a broken rooftop, a storm can thump a tree on it, various harms can occur that need the quick consideration of a house sitter.

In this way, there you have the reason you have to select house sitters to help your business adventure. There are vast amounts of reasons why somebody may require somebody to look out for their property, and you can profit by this.

You remain to profit when you think carefully and begin a house sitting business. You can be rounding up the batter in a matter of moments and giving incredible support of your customers too.

The housesitting business is a territory that has been disregarded for quite a while yet you can benefit from it in case you're set up to go out on a limb and adventure out alone.

Sitter Services - Finding Babysitters Made Easy

Discovering great sitter administrations are troublesome nowadays. While not all sitters are awful, there will dependably be that sitter you'll pay eight dollars an hour to sit on your lounge chair while your children watch kid's shows and after that, you'll get back home to a house that appears as though a tornado hit it. You'll be fortunate to discover a sitter that will ensure the house is cleaner toward the night's end than it was the point at which she arrived.

Honestly, these days it is elusive a sitter, particularly a youngster. This may be because adolescents are never again keen on profiting because their folks are giving them cash or life's anything but difficult to drop by. This may likewise be because they're calendar is pressed with school responsibilities, or guardians don't think its excellent utilization of their high school kids' time. Or then again youngsters are too occupied with "tweeting" their life on Twitter or "labeling" their companions with the most recent occasion on Facebook.

A decent sitter administration turns out to be considerably harder to discover with all the work you need to do to enlist a sitter. You need to inquire as to whether they know any sitter or post advertisements on school and Red Cross notices. What's more, in case you're lucky somebody reacted to your hunt, regardless you need to do some fundamental estimates like individual verifications for any criminal records. You even need to complete a character to verify whether the individual is genuinely fit to keep an eye on children. With every one of these things that you have to do, you'll be very depleted even before you get depleted.

The useful thing on the web sitter administrations is promptly accessible these days. Its notoriety has become significantly over the previous years and is rapidly turning into the favored technique for guardians to locate the ideal sitter for their family. With various babysitting sites with a large number of sitters to browse, it's a quick and advantageous approach to discover sitters in your general vicinity. You'll find a sitter that flawlessly coordinates your family needs in a matter of seconds. What's more, by giving sitter profiles, evaluations, tributes from guardians, and a day in and day out open communication framework, it will merely involve minutes before you discover extraordinary and reliable sitters directly in your neighborhood would love to look out for your little ones. Finding a decent sitter has never been simpler.

The most effective method to Run a Property Management Business

A property the board business is truly encouraging today, so it is a sign for you to think about it as another business for your needs. If you might want to maintain this business for your needs, there are a few stages you should know so you will utilize them as the best assistance for you. To find out about those ways, it is better for you to look at this section will direct you to make the best decision for your needs.

The initial step you have to consider is to possess a brought together area to direct business. For this situation, it will be a smart thought for you to pick the suitable spot that is extraordinarily key so it will bolster your business great. To make your industry progressively prevalent, you can consider moving to a company fabricating so you can put your business on the map.

The subsequent stage you should know is to keep up associations with individual contractual workers and pros. If you can keep up its relationship, you will have more associates who will help you in maintaining your business high. It implies that they could take your administration while required, so it very well may be a decent advantage for you.

At that point, it is likewise better to set up your fund. For this situation, it is prompted for you to open a financial balance for an independent company so you can make sure that it will be helpful for you. By having this sparing record, you will most likely separate your very own fund with the money of your business so you can utilize it admirably. By doing this thing, you will most likely keep away from the terrible things that can occur into your business so you can bolster it to develop well, and it will be favorable for you.

Analyzing Your eBay Sales

Here are few hints on the best way to examine your eBay sales:

1. When loads of unsold things torment you, you have to get deliberate and do some examination. Figuring your sell-through rate (STR) is essential for all vendors. STR is the proportion of things offered available to be purchased in a given period partitioned by the quantity of those things that sold. If you provided ten stuff on Sunday and four of them sold, your STR is 40 percent.

2. It is likewise essential to ascertain the average sale price (ASP) of the things that sold. Include the sale price of the considerable number of things that sold in a specific period - multi-day, a month, a year, etc. Try not to stress over Final Value Fees or Insertion Fees. You are just worried about the gross sale price. Partition the aggregate by the number sold. When you sold five sets of gloves for $15, $12, $9, $9, and $8, your complete is $53, and your ASP is $10.60.

3. When you have determined your STR and ASP, pose yourself a few inquiries. Are a few things only difficult to sell? Would you be able to sell more when you included more photographs or featured your sales?

4. Make a note of the brand names, hues, and kinds of things that have the most noteworthy STR. Concentrate on

structure your stock of those things, and don't buy the ones with low STRs.

5. Focus on the STR for specific things as well as for the class in which you generally sell as often as possible. It tends to be repetitive to examine a complete classification when you don't have extraordinary programming that takes the necessary steps for you. However, you can complete a harsh estimate. Include the number of sales in a page loaded with finished exchanges in a classification. At that point tally what amount of the sales prices are exhibited in green - these are the ones that sold. The red ones are unsold things. Complete a few pages worth of results, and ascertain the proportion of sales to the number of finished exchanges. The outcomes are the sell-through rate.

By examining your eBay sales, you will probably settle on better choices in your business with the goal that will almost certainly benefit more over the long haul.

Selling Through Etsy

Guidelines are accessible for you to pursue to enable you to expand your sales through Etsy.

Guideline #1

You can't only begin a shop and would whatever you like to d with it. Be dependable.

Guideline #2

Customers won't most likely observe your genuine items, so setting numerous photos in various edges will enable them to choose to acquire the item. Make sure to have it centered.

Guideline #3

Prices ought to be on fixed-rate, don't overprice your items, overpriced items are challenging to sell.

Guideline #4

Make exceptional items; purchasers will disparage your question when they think that it is delightful. Go for exciting things to have it effectively sold.

Guideline #5

Customize your shop; one of the least demanding approaches to help sales is to improve the appearance and data accessible on your site.

Guideline #6

Make a blog, utilize a blog to drive individuals into your Etsy shop, and educate past and potential clients about what you are arranging and what you are making.

Guideline #7

Offer a sale or markdown to build consciousness of your items.

Guideline #8

Join an Etsy gathering, joining a group can enable you to advance your items.

Selling on Etsy may not be as simple as in the past, but rather certainly these tips or guidelines can enable you to support your confidence and in particular your promoting strategies, so never surrender with something you want to do. When there's a will, there is dependably away. Also, an issue can never be known as an issue when it has no arrangements.

With regards to selling on the web, the following eBay is Etsy and selling on Etsy has turned into the enormous pooch when selling natively constructed items. Try not to be forgotten from the rest or waste your time marketing on a stage that doesn't take into account the custom made line.

Web Business Tips - How Can I Increase Sales of Fiverr Gigs?

There are numerous techniques with which the part can increment Fiverr gig sales -

1. Discover every one of your capacities and make a rundown. You can likewise give an alluring depiction to the majority of your gigs with photos. You can post these on this site.

2. Check the necessities of the general population on the message sheets of various social promoting destinations. As you as of now have caused an introduction for your gig all you to need to do is to speak with the invested individual and discover his necessity, and you can advance your introduction to the concerned party. If they like the

presentation, they will consent to profit your administrations.

3. Post your administrations on free grouped promotion destinations offering your administrations. The individual who is keen on your administrations will get in touch with you.

4. Search through the necessity segment of different gatherings and networks where the individuals have publicized their prerequisites. You can connect with them through this channel and give the introduction of your administrations. If they like the presentation, you may land the position.

5. Solicit the client care from Fiverr site about how you can feature your gig on the first page of the site with the goal that more individuals will see it and call you in regards to your concert.

6. Work back connections on different web journals, gatherings, networks, and other website pages. It is one of the smart thoughts for expanding the sales of the gig.

These are just a portion of the ways with which the individuals from the Fiverr.com can elevate his gig to individuals around the globe who visit this site, and increment the sale and subsequently his very own salary from the introduction. These were only a couple of web business tips. Anyway, gigs are the following huge things around the bend.

How to Be a Great Portrait Photographer

Photography is a champion among the most captivating part-times and callings on the planet. There is in no way like catching sections of life and safeguarding it on film. There are numerous kinds of photography, yet a standout amongst the most prominent is representation photography for use in the studio or at capacity, for example, a wedding.

An excellent photograph representation is depicted as an image with a quality picture that catches both the real highlights and character of the individual. Finding great movies is incredibly testing because a photographer needs a subject with a playful style that additionally reflects affectability and uniqueness.

There are bunches of components that photography aficionados need to know in catching the ideal representation. For an image to be viewed as excellent, it must find at any rate one part that demonstrates the highlights and character of the subject just as one that shows his or her distinction. The image must uncover a significant piece of the people's personality that can be recognizable by the individuals who know them. In this manner, it is tough for representation to demonstrate the character of the subject when they have met for them just because.

The photograph shoot, regardless of whether in the studio or out on the area, should start when the subject is glad and quiet with his or her appearance and environment. Never shoot if the item is apprehensive or on edge since it will reflect in the photos. Prop the discussions up when shooting begins since it as a rule keeps the subject progressively loose.

Keep in mind that the subject does not have to grin to make the picture look great. Frequently, an insightful or useful articulation is favored since it catches a higher amount of people's character. This is significant since the photographer assumes responsibility for a photograph session. The subject must feel that the individual behind the camera comprehends what he's doing and is experienced enough to advise the individual how to present. The photographer himself must be readied and quiet all through the session.

Most likely, the best light that can be utilized for catching the character of the subject is average sunshine. The assortment of lighting decisions achieved by open-air conditions gives progressively inventive conceivable outcomes for the photographer. It is having the issue sit close to the window can likewise deliver significant impacts. The main impediment of natural light is that it's not always predictable. This is the reason all photographers must use artificial lighting. All photographers must have studio flashes. Likewise, the situation of the photographer in connection to the subject can also be moved to augment the light accessible. Delivering the ideal picture may appear to be troublesome at first; however, by experimentation, you will pick up learning to enable you to prevail with regards to turning into a top-notch representation photographer.

Chapter six

Vocation As a Wedding Photographer

Individuals these days are thinking about vocations in different fields which a significant number of us didn't consider prior. One of such areas is professional wedding photography. There were photographers prior too. More individuals are thinking about to move toward becoming professionals around here. Professional photography isn't just about having a propelled camera and clicking pictures. It takes long stretches of training and tolerance to turn into a decent professional photographer.

Wedding photography, as the name itself proposes, includes shooting a wedding function alongside the occasions occurring when it also. Turning into a professional wedding photographer needs enthusiasm and ability. Wedding photographer catches the enchanted snapshots of your vast day which you will treasure deep-rooted with loved ones.

Wedding photography is to be sure a vital piece of any wedding event. Couples arranging their weddings do keep a different spending plan alongside every other course of action. It very well may be a cost which gives you longterm esteem if you procure a specialist professional photographer.

Individuals who have a robust enthusiasm for photography are currently considering to end up professional marriage photographers. With regards to taking pictures, these photographers ensure that the images they catch are immaculate and show the feelings and emotions. It can regularly demonstrate to challenge and including task. Wedding photographers ought to have different interpersonal characteristics as they need to manage the visitors on occasion.

Before picking a wedding photographer, individuals check different things and afterward observe whether the individual matches the prerequisite or not. This incorporates photography style, aptitude, character, and so forth. The spending limit is additionally one of the criteria for individuals picking such professionals. They might want to get an incentive for their cash as opposed to merely spending heaps of money for the wedding. There is a particular strain to give the best outcomes around here. When you convey the best, at that point, this business can be remunerating also.

Practically all wedding photographers are capable clients of cutting edge types of gear. In any case, just the professional one's expertise to utilize them suitably to catch the best feelings. As each wedding photographer has their very own style of photography, it is necessary for the general population contracting their administrations to realize what sort of style they need. When you are uncertain which style would suit you the best, give doing some examination and locate a shot about the different forms of photography and instances of them. You can likewise request that the professional show you photos of his/her past work. This would give you a thought of what you would need for your enormous day.

The arrangement ought to be done in highly contrasting. This implies you ought to have an understanding marked between both the gatherings. Ensure you notice every one of the focuses that you talked about and consent to it.

Wedding photography is such artistry, which you can ace after adequate practice. It is a difficult calling. However, whenever done the correct way, can be remunerating also. It's not just about taking pictures. It's tied in with making recollections.

The best strategy to Make Money Online Writing and Selling eBooks

To compose eBooks, you should make sense of what you know and write as if addressing others. It's not too troublesome, and if you have ever produced a paper for a school task, you have every one of the requirements as of now. You don't need to be specialist on your eBook subject, even though it helps, as most data can be discovered on the web and in your nearby library. You don't need to be a decent author as most word processors have language and spell checking instruments.

Today, any eBook can be sold on the Internet; here are the most popular sports with the most significant amounts of open interest.

"Step by step instructions to" eBooks

Aides and manuals that disclose how to do different things and how to tackle various issues, similar to how to profit on the web, how to advance site, and so forth.

Business eBooks

They disclose how to begin, account, oversee, create, or advance you're on the web or disconnected business and give tips, guidance, procedures, and diagrams for progress.

Home/Family

These eBooks give data to family about issues, for example, cooking, plans, youngsters and child-rearing, planting, finishing, pets, marriage, home improvement, and land.

PC related

These eBooks give instructional exercises and direction on subjects like programming dialects, web planning, PC equipment, designs, and the sky is the limit from there.

Cash/Jobs

digital books in this class give controls on themes like an obligation, the board, training, independent work, cash making opportunities, investments, enterprise, locally situated organizations, account, and employment.

Society/Culture

These eBooks class spread subjects like unknown dialects, legislative issues, government, craftsmanship, love life, travel, theory, religion, science, and the sky is the limit from there.

Specialized eBooks

Concentrate on specialized subjects like hardware, building, mechanics, and so forth.

Fiction eBooks

Books, short stories, verse, sentiment, sensual writing, dream, and so forth.

Ability/Talent eBooks

Show you the essentials and propelled systems of ability related recreations, pastimes or sports, similar to chess, enchantment, poker, photography, golf, and so on.

Wellbeing eBooks

Disclose how to fix different infections, sicknesses, or conditions and give medicinal data and appeal to improve wellbeing.

Greeting Cards For A Home Based Business

In this time where the economy is confronting an overall bedlam, numerous individuals have more than only one activity to have the option to support their money related needs and to make a decent living. There are likewise some that pick to wander in business since they accept that accomplishment regarding budgetary is simpler accomplish when you are in the business world. Command post business is well known among individuals who wish to increase additional pay. One of the numerous organizations that individuals are getting into is making welcome cards at the solace of their own home.

Welcome cards are the most well known and the least complicated approach to express an individual's sentiments and contemplations for their affection. What's more, even though there are numerous ways these days to send and state how you feel through the web, many individuals still consideration to composing and postcards. This is the reason making cards is a hit. Beside the way that it is anything but difficult to make and the materials are promptly accessible in the stores, you can likewise do it in the solace of your own home with the assistance of your relatives.

For individuals who are masterfully disposed making cards will be as simple as a bit of cake however when you are figuring how to cause welcome cards in the event that you to don't have the ability of making one, at that point need not stress there are destinations in the web where you can gain proficiency with the specialty of making beautiful and one of a kind welcome cards. You can likewise peruse craftsmanship books for you to create incredible plans for your welcome cards. The beat of all is to give your creative mind and inventiveness a chance to work. When you have your thoughts as the main priority, you would now be able to chip away at making business-like cards that you can sell. In selling, you can either acquaint it with your companions or create your very own online locales and highlight your tickets there. Joining bazaars and fairs will likewise help advance your business and meet possible and future clients.

Getting into welcome card making business won't only use your salary yet, also, will enable you to improve your inventiveness and creative mind. It is additionally a decent method to acquire additional cash without living the four corners of your home and be with your affection ones and also connected with them in an action that is both fun and produces pay.

Everybody Can Sell Art Online

Online craftsmanship deals may have once been the domain of significant exhibition halls and displays, yet this isn't the situation in the present online artistry showcase. Developing significantly, the online artistry commercial center is no longer as hard to enter as it was in earlier years, and anybody can set up a shop, site, online exhibition profile, or blog and sell craftsmanship online to clients who are experiencing all around the globe. You don't should be a craftsman to sell your specialty in a web-based setting, and you could be a vendor, broker, or somebody who is an authority and is hoping to start exchanging a portion of the compelling artwork works in your accumulation. Exhibitions and other more prominent organizations still sell craftsmanship on the web; however, they are never again the leading players on the field.

One reason that it has turned out to be simpler than any time in recent memory to sell artistry online is something many refer to as SEO, also called Search Engine

Optimization. In the past, when web search tools were less refined, and the web was a much less aggressive spot, all you needed to do was make a site and trust that individuals will discover you. This is not true anymore, and there are present things that you can do to enable your website, to blog, or online store seem higher up in the aftereffects of significant web indexes like Google, Yahoo, and Bing. The more substantial part of these include the utilization of catchphrases in your portrayals; in the event that you are selling contemporary workmanship, at that point "contemporary craftsmanship" ought to be referenced a period or two in your site's depiction, in the title, and in the content portraying the workmanship available to be purchased. It very well may be more confounded than this, yet put SEO is essential to your prosperity if you need to sell artistry on the web, regardless of your identity.

Putting craftsmanship online available to be purchased is something that artisans, artistry darlings, and representatives would all be able to do easily because of devices like blogging, online craftsmanship exhibition/commercial center profiles, and web-based life systems. These things make it simpler than at any other time to set up a nearness for your business and your specialty on the internet and get yourself and your work out there in a matter of seconds by any stretch of the imagination. Regardless of your identity or what your craft foundation may resemble you can sell artistry on the web, so why not begin today?

Providing food Business

Offering an outstanding administration, the nourishment which is served by a providing food business is noteworthy because in addition to the fact that it is scrumptious brilliantly introduced also. Although there are many providing food organizations, there are some which have some expertise in specific capacities, for example, a meeting.

A gathering offers a business a perfect chance to show to visitors that their administrations ought to be picked. A meeting additionally empowers a company the opportunity to connect with different organizations. When senior partners inside an organization visit and meet potential customers up close and personal, this offers them the perfect opportunity to convey a constructive message since they are in charge of conversing with their customers. As a gathering ought to be fruitful, a business must ensure that the sustenance which is served to their visitors is heavenly and of the most astounding quality.

Providing food business will contemplate the kind of nourishment that their clients need. If a gathering has just welcomed an insignificant number of individuals, setting up an enormous measure of nourishment will be pointless. Nonetheless, if several visitors are expected to go to a gathering, a providing food business will probably make enough nourishment. The sort of nourishment which will be served ought to likewise be advised to a providing food business too. If hot sustenance is required, it tends to be arranged either on location or at various premises. This relies upon whether the scene which is facilitating a meeting has enormous enough kitchen offices or not. Notwithstanding, if cold sustenance is required, it tends to be set up nearby because the main machine which might be necessary is an ice chest.

Just as a meeting, a cooking business can likewise serve sustenance at birthday parties. All things considered, gatherings are a period of festivity, much association ought to be done as such that it is entirely pleasant. When lone grown-ups visit, the general population who are facilitating the gathering should ensure that enough liquor has been acquired. Notwithstanding the refreshments which visitors can drink, sumptuous sustenance ought to be served, which will most likely mollify any craving.

In contrast to formal meetings and meals, bites and finger sustenances can be served at a birthday party. Frankfurter moves, sandwiches and delectable cakes are only a portion of the numerous things of nutrition which can be set up by an expert providing food business. As the general population who are sorting out a gathering might not have enough available time to plan nourishment themselves, a cooking business will offer true serenity because not exclusively will sustenance be served yet it will be flavorful too.

As the costs which are charged by a providing food business are entirely reasonable, it is suggested that statements from numerous organizations are looked for some time before a gathering occurs. In this manner, both the most ideal cost and nourishment will be picked. As cooking organizations have their very own site, a statement can be found in a flash just as what sorts of occasions they provide food and the kinds of nourishment they serve.

Chapter seven

Earn A Living Buying and Selling Domain Names

Selling domain names can be an enormous income maker in case you're ready to find and sell domain names that have a high volume of traffic or that are straightforwardly identified with a popular item or administration. These domain names can make thousands for their proprietors with almost no exertion. There are numerous accounts even right up 'til the present time where the clearance of separate domain names delivered a considerablele number of dollars in benefit. This business isn't just for experienced webmasters; anybody with a little learning can make a steady income purchase and selling domain names. This part will give you the data you have to benefit in this business using a simple to pursue control.

The main thing you have to do is discover a word on a web crawler, for instance, Google that is very utilized and scans for a word that isn't utilized by numerous sites. The best apparatus to look would purchase a watchword analyzer. The reason you would need to buy this program as opposed to using free analyzers is that the paid forms are refreshed all the more as often as possible, so they show progressively precise outcomes and lets you know of all the challenge you're facing with your catchphrases.

Now you will need to make a site for your domain name, and it could be straightforward. Compose an article identified with your catchphrase utilizing a simple word record and spare the document as an HTML. Once your site is discharged to the world, you should concentrate on structure the destinations traffic to get exceptional and different watchers. Presently you should present your website on any free locales, for example, grouped advertisements or registries. you'll need to fire up connection exchange with different sites. You can do this by messaging the website admin or finding a connection exchange arrange that enables webmasters to exchange joins with one another.

You objective presently is to keep working up your connections until you get a good progression of traffic and in the long run, you'll get your site and domain recorded in all the real web indexes. If your rating is right you can discover a domain name appraiser to perceive how much your name is worth so, all things considered, you can choose whether you need to sell it or keep expanding the domain names rankings.

Acquire Extra Cash Proofreading and Editing For Online Companies

There is snappy cash to be made on the web. If you need to gain additional money from home, basically by utilizing the internet, your decisions are perpetual. One of the more prominent jobs online that are being sent to specialists who work at home is editing and altering.

There are such a large number of web businesses making sites day by day that they can't stay aware of the substance. The substance is re-appropriated to an independent author yet will at present be edited and altered before being put nearby.

You can procure additional money, offering your administrations to organizations that need your assistance. The interest is fantastic for editors and straightforward editors. You needn't bother with a degree, only a solid handle of the English language and the capacity to spot incorrectly spelled words, divided sentences, and have the option to decide whether something is lucid or not.

Editors can have work sent to them day by day, week by week, or month to month contingent upon the amount they need to work. There is no more straightforward method to procure additional money for somebody who wants to peruse. The undertakings are necessary and don't take much time. Most of the substance will be in articles that are under 700 words.

You should open an online record; for example, PayPal so installment can be sent to you securely and safely by the customer. The settled upon sum will be moved to your paper once work has been finished and conveyed effectively.

When you have wrecked, there is no compelling reason to freeze most customers will give you another shot in the wake of clarifying what wasn't right. If you demonstrate yourself to be relevant to the customer, at that point, your capacity to gain additional money will be constant. Most customers will keep a couple of good editors so once you are in, you are in.

Starting a YouTube Channel

Beginning a YouTube channel to advertise your business, item, administration, or ability is an extraordinary way to assemble social value. When you construct a multitude of supporters on YouTube, the group of spectators will be sensitive to whatever recordings you share, and you can utilize this to further your potential benefit.

In less than one year you can amass a million endorsers of your YouTube channel. Consider that for a moment and attempt to grasp the size of that promoting power. If you have a million people bought into your channel and you post another video, you will probably have 100,000 perspectives immediately. If you bundle a message into the video about your business, item, administration, or ability, you will end up being a web sensation and bring home the bacon in the meantime.

There are numerous stars on YouTube that are bringing home the bacon from YouTube alone yet there are additionally numerous individuals who are bringing back the bacon from their YouTube profit just as the benefit from other salary identified with their YouTube channel. You can gain cash from the YouTube partner program when Google ads show up in your recordings and to the side of your records. You can likewise acquire some money by setting joins on your site for watchers to tap on so they can visit your different business locales.

An extraordinary way to get traffic to your channel is through article showcasing. You can likewise develop a base of supporters by having a Twitter record and building a following. In any case, the quickest way to create a base of endorsers on YouTube is to have great substance. Your recordings will possibly turn into a web sensation if you wow your crowd.

How to Build Wealth

It isn't difficult to build individual wealth. A few people have the misinterpretation of getting to be wealthy. Wealth may mean a lot of things for various people. Monetarily, wealth is necessarily a blend of financial success and increasing physical assets.

This may likewise mean fewer liabilities and more reserve funds.

If that is the depiction of wealth, at that point be glad since you have ways on the best way to build wealth particularly in these difficult times. A standout amongst the ideal means to begin your wealth building program is to contribute your money on assets.

There are numerous favorable circumstances in putting your money on assets. May this be on real estate, financial investments or a business, you will have more unique opportunities to build your wealth than in some other methods. It gives you the suspicion that all is well and good that the money you contribute will likewise harvest twofold the sum you put in.

Also, because the profits are stunning, you will perceive any reason why a lot of people incline toward this wealth building framework. To comprehend this more, investigate some ways to contribute to assets as one of your wealth building strategies:

Business: One of the ideal ways on the most proficient method to build wealth is by discovering intends to continue a relentless stream of income into your pocket. How would you do this? You can go into the business that will bring regular income into your record. Having a company that keeps on developing and thrive will empower you to pay for your costs, obligations, set aside extra cash and re-put this in different methods.

Real Estate: This is one physical asset that increases in value after some time. This is likely why a lot of people are contributing to real estate mainly when the business sectors are low since they can exchange this for a higher sum than what they got it for.

This is a long haul investment, and you may most likely not see the profits immediately. When you are genuine in your wealth building program, at that point the holding up period would not be quite a bit of an issue to you. The vast majority who put resources into real estate more often than not has an eye for really great properties and can predict the ascent in the estimation of these properties over the years. To find out about this, you ought to effectively do your exploration and concentrate the patterns of the business.

Investments: Whether it is in stocks, bonds or values, contributing to financial or paper assets is an extraordinary way to go. It is a type of easy revenue that does not take the majority of your time but instead will, in any case, create a generous measure of profits.

You can likewise put your money on mutual funds, foreign exchange, and gold. Before you put in your investments, ensure you think about the financial trade first. Find out about the patterns and research on high stocks and bonds to put resources into.

If you are not ready to deal with this without anyone else's input, request the counsel and help of a reserve supervisor that can enable you to allow your funds better and twofold your profits.

Demonstrated Strategies on How to Build Wealth

When the economy is so unsteady, numerous people are finding a hard time building individual wealth. It isn't outlandish. Regardless of how troublesome times can be, you can, in any case, make your wealth, if you realize how to play your cards right.

There are numerous strategies on how to build wealth. If you would look on the web, there are lots of plans, jobs, investment and business openings that will make an individual's income. To expand your income would mean a lot to your wealth building program. This will allow you to spare more and carry on with the sort of way of life you need.

How to do this? There are a ton of approaches to do this, however, to rearrange the means, here are some demonstrated wealth building strategies, that can enable you to achieve the highest point of your financial objectives:

1. Lucrative Job. A lucrative career has its numerous advantages. There is that expansive pay, significant assets, benefits and the chance to possess a stock inside your organization. It might sound simple. However, this methodology takes a lot of hard work.

More often than not, you don't land that lucrative position immediately. The key here is to discover your interests, your aptitudes and transform it into gold. Try not to squander your time in jobs that you know nothing about or have no enthusiasm for. Concentrate on a career that will enable you to develop, learn and get advanced.

Be energetic with what you do and grow great expert connections. This is how you get to a six-figure pay through a worthwhile profession.

2. Organizations. Consider something you can do that will reply to people's needs. This is the start of business though. To finish it off, this must be something important to you; else, you may lose heart when difficulties arise.

A business is an incredible way to build your wealth since it resembles watching out for a homestead that can enable you to gather money. Just consider it like this - it resembles planting a seed which speaks to the hard work you put into the administrations and items you give to your clients and once they're ready for the picking, you need to read them and place it in the capacity.

If you are chosen in building your wealth, at that point, you should start conceptualizing a business plan now.

3. Financial Investments. This incorporates stocks, securities, mutual funds, values, foreign exchange, and some more. Contributing to these paper assets will enable you to build wealth quick since it gives a way to procure easy revenue. This implies separated from your job and your business, you can win a lot of money notwithstanding sitting at home or in your office by contributing to these paper assets.

4. Bank Savings. This is one of the wealth-building strategies that don't mean creating an income yet will have a significant job in building wealth. Sparing a segment of your income will add to your liquid assets that you can use for crises, costs and other future needs.

Sparing your money through the bank has its advantages as well, such as procuring a little measure of enthusiasm after some time. Ordinary stores to your bank is an extraordinary propensity to set up mainly if you are not kidding in building individual wealth.

Might you want to make sense of how to create wealth without having any money to contribute? Do you think this is conceivable? In all actuality, you are undoubtedly ready to create wealth without spending a dime and how this function is by merely exploiting the distinctive conceivable outcomes that the Internet brings to the table. Numerous people don't think about it and dependably expect that when another person says, that it is difficult to accomplish something that is an established truth.

The Internet has numerous conceivable outcomes for you to exploit to start creating wealth without spending any money. You have something in your own that is more valuable than money with regards to investing and this one thing is your time. By merely investing your time you will almost certainly produce a consistent income that is going to enable you to create the wealth that you are looking for.

If you're willing to contribute your time, at that point all you will need to do is go on the Internet and start getting progressively acquainted with it. There will be numerous chances and programs that you can browse yet the one thing that you need to ensure you do is that you do what's required research to observe a program that will be genuine and that won't vanish on you.

The reason you need to ensure you do this is that in such a significant number of cases people have lost a lot of their time because the program truly vanishes after they have joined. You certainly don't need this to happen to you, and you need to ensure that you have a plan that is going to stick around with the goal for you to get rewarded on your time and exertion.

Instructions to Create Wealth Without Having a Huge Capital to Start With

OK prefer to make sense of how to make riches without having huge money, to begin with? This is a champion among the most critical destinations for someone to have the ability to achieve when they begin their calling on the Internet. Not many individuals know accurately how to manage respects to the beginning without having a large proportion of cash to contribute.

Here is the well-ordered technique for structure wealth without having a considerable capital:

#1 Join An Affordable Network Marketing Online Opportunity

The underlying advance that you have to take will be to join a moderate system marketing on the web opportunity. This will be a critical step since you need to ensure the opportunity is genuine, offers a valuable service and in the meantime is reasonable because you would prefer not to spend a lot of your money into keeping up your opportunity. The way to finding a decent chance that is moderate will be to concentrate on doing your exploration on the various open doors before settling on an official conclusion.

#2 Master Article Marketing And Use It To Promote Your Business

Article marketing is a ground-breaking limited time method that enables you to begin without contributing any money whatsoever. All you will do is investing your time so it will be imperative for you to ace article marketing and have it be your essential, limited time method to expand your business results.

#3 Increase Your Profits And Then Start Investing More Into The Business

By acing article marketing, you are going to expand your benefits before investing a lot of money into your business. This is for what reason will be imperative for you to ace step 2. Extending your benefits before spending a lot of money on your business will be one of the most astute moves to make.

Creating Wealth Without Investing Any Money

Might you want to make sense of how to create wealth without investing any money? By proceeding to peruse this section, you're going to discover precisely how to start building wealth without putting any money somewhere near merely going on the Internet and being presented to the numerous ways that you can use to get this going.

Creating wealth is one of the numerous objectives that people have at the top of the priority list with regards to producing a consistent income for what's to come. A great many people need to do this yet have no money at transfer to have the capacity to begin. Everyone feels that to create wealth you need money to put and this might be valid as a rule yet now, and again all you will need to do is contribute your time.

The Internet offers numerous open doors that you can exploit by just investing your time and along these lines you can start producing an income that you set aside to begin creating your wealth. Additionally, this income can fill in as extra cash that you can put again into the opportunity that you're exploited to develop it more. Remember that in the end, you will need to put money into your business yet not in the first place.

Is it true that you will dedicate time on low maintenance premise to develop your business gradually? If the appropriate response is indeed, at that point, you have the correct attitude to have the capacity to start creating wealth by using the diverse methods that the Internet brings to the table. The one thing that you will need to do is dedicate time to finding that ideal income opportunity that is going to enable you to accomplish your objective. The main three essential factors that you need to ensure this opportunity has is reasonable, genuine and offers a valuable service on the Internet. By providing that it fits this depiction you're going to realize that is an opportunity that won't vanish on you.

CONCLUSION

The credit crunch has cut down numerous business mammoths and in the process the loss of multiple employment. If you are one of the influenced people and you are pondering what next, here is a business idea that will knock your socks off. The standard for most businesses is that you need money to make money. Indeed, this could be consistent with some degree yet what of those people who have no cash-flow to try and begin a private venture? Telling this person, they ought to leave to destiny will lie; you can make money online without spending a solitary dime. Google has one such business opportunity where all you require is to have a blog. All you will do is put some posting on your website pages at that point register with Google AdSense for nothing. Google will feel free to place adverts on your blog that are identified with your posting. Declarations exist of people who make a great many dollars from Google AdSense. The different business idea is to select with affiliate promoting programs like Amazon. Being a partner with Amazon is gratis. When you enlist load their connections onto your blog, any individual who pursues this connection and buy an item, Amazon will pay you a commission. Register with these business programs and afterward discover ways of directing people to your business and you will be in business. Use was showcasing strategies which are likewise free, a portion of these promoting procedures incorporate presenting your business connects on catalogs, ordered publicizing site or selecting viral advertising programs like traffic digger.

www.ingramcontent.com/pod-product-compliance
Lightning Source LLC
Chambersburg PA
CBHW030723220526
45463CB00005B/2154